FUNNY STORIES

CONTAINS STORY FULL OF COMEDIES AND FUN!

PRATYUSH HIMANSHU

Made with ♥ on the Notion Press Platform
www.notionpress.com

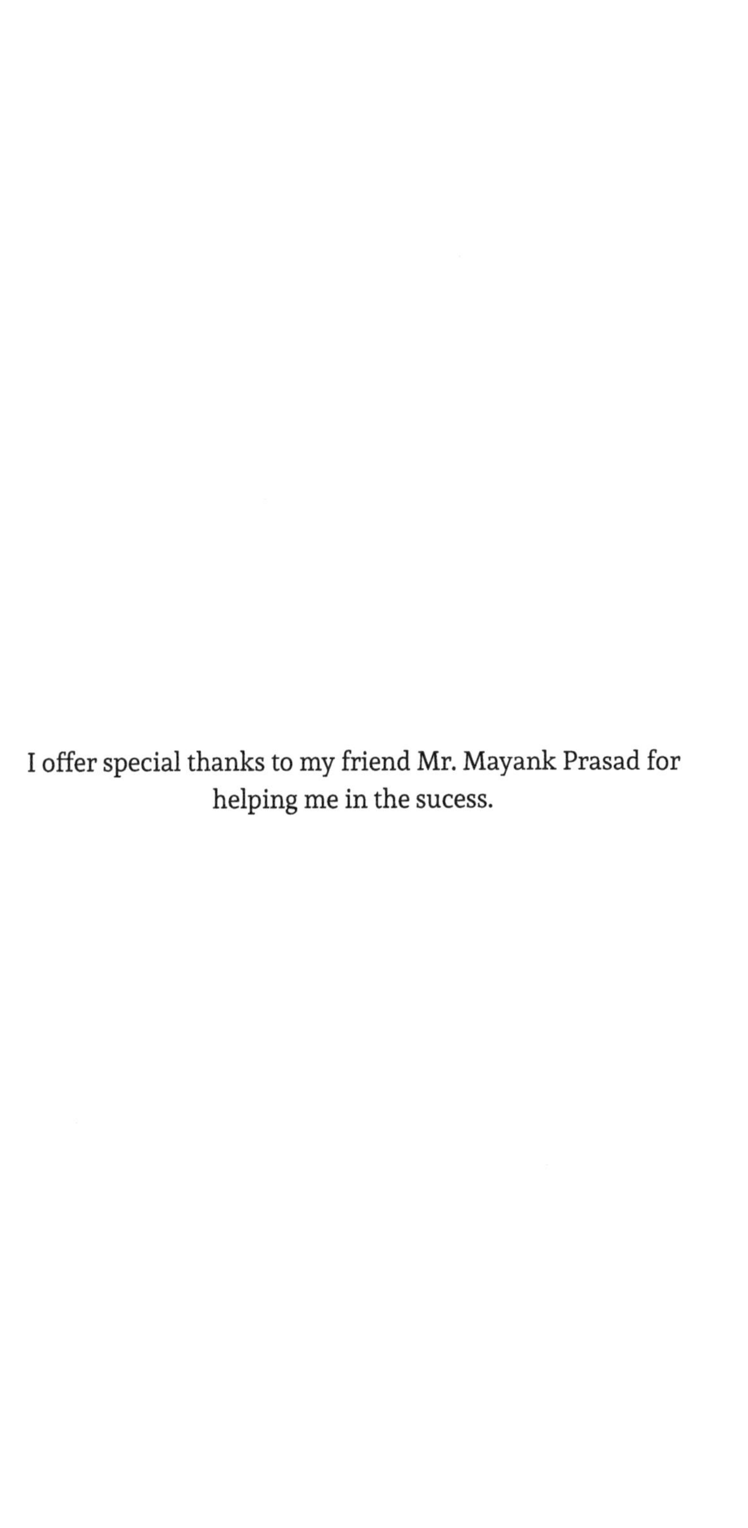
I offer special thanks to my friend Mr. Mayank Prasad for helping me in the sucess.

Contents

Preface

First of all, stories are the most important and easiest way to express your thoughts. It also brings joy to our life. Funny stories bring joy and fun to our life. If a person is stressed or sad then he can read and then he can read these story books.

Acknowledgements

Mr. Mayank Prasad

Mr. Aditya Himanshu

Mr. RVK Himanshu

Ms. Rima Himanshu

Prologue

There are many characters in this story which will be a surprise.

The children will be filling the page with their favsite characters in this story.

1

The Missing Tenth Man

0.1

Ten men go to the Ganges one day to dip in the holy Indian river. They hold hands with each other while taking the dip. But they somehow forget to hold hands while coming out of the water.

After coming to the shore, one of the senior men asks, “Have we all crossed the river safely?” The remaining men start looking at each other. They are confused.

Now the senior man asks everyone to lift their hand up take a count. He starts counting and takes a count of each person.

When the count stops at nine, other men start screaming. They even go looking for the missing tenth man. This goes on with each person counting men up to nine and missing the tenth man.

A cap vendor, who keeps watching the amusing scene, offers help. The vendor gives a cap to each man and asks them to wear it. The men are confused as to what is happening. The vendor asks the senior man to gather all the caps, including his own, and count them all.

Everyone is surprised and happy to see ten caps. The silly men credit the vendor for have helped them find their missing member and believe it to be magic. The vendor charges a good amount for each cap and happily walks away.

But what has happened? The men forgot to count themselves; hence, the number was always nine.

2

We are even

One day, Nasreddin Hodja goes to a Turkish bath. As he is offered an old towel and a robe, he is upset that nobody is paying attention to him. He says nothing but leaves a hefty tip at the counter while returning.

A week later, he goes back and is very well received this time. He is given the royal treatment and is also provided extra services. Hodja is happy but hardly leaves any tips.

0.2

Everyone is surprised and curious to know why Hodja left just a small tip this time.

He says, "Today's tip is for the services offered during the last visit. And the tip given then was for today. We are even now."

3

Frog and his belly burst

Two frogs — father and son — live together in a pond. One day, the son frog was playing in a garden when he spots a cow. He returns to the pond and tells his father that he saw a giant scary monster.

The father frog does not believe it and tries to rubbish it away. When the kid insists, the father pays attention, and the son frog starts to explain how big the 'giant' was.

0.3

The father frog fills up the air in his stomach and asks him if the monster looked like that? The son says, “No, it is much bigger.” The father fills up some more air in his belly and asks the son if the giant was that big. The son says no again.

The father does it again and again until his belly becomes huge with air. Before he could ask the question, his belly bursts. The father starts crying out in pain.

4

A man and three thugs

In a faraway village, a man used to help a landlord without asking for anything in return. He was extremely superstitious. Impressed with the work, the landlord rewards the man with a big healthy goat, one day.

The man carries the goat on his shoulders and starts walking back home. Three wicked thugs observe him and decide to trick him.

The first thug comes to him and asks, "Why are you carrying a dog on your shoulders." The man gets angry and tells the thug that it is a goat and not a dog.

As he keeps walking, the second thug passes by and enquires why he was carrying a dead calf on his shoulders. The man's anger multiplies and says, "You fool! Can't you see this is a goat?" However, the second thug's question plants the seed of suspicion in the man's mind.

After walking for some more distance, the third thug approaches the man, and asks in a sarcastic tone, "Why are you carrying a donkey on your shoulders?"

The superstitious man gets scared thinking the goat is actually a ghost. He leaves it right there and runs away.

The three thugs take the goat away, laughing at the man's stupidity.

0.4

5

Sandwiches for Dinner

Two friends, who are advocates, visit a restaurant and order drinks.

0.5

They do not order anything to eat as they have a sandwich each in their briefcases. The advocates take out their sandwiches and start eating them.

The waiter comes, and sternly says, “You are not allowed to eat your own sandwiches inside the restaurant.”

The smart friends look at each other, laugh, and exchange their sandwiches.

6

Age of the leg

An old man visits a doctor to seek a

Enter Caption

remedy for the terrible pain in his leg. The doctor replies saying, “I am sorry but this could be due to your old age.” He further explains why nothing can be done to help with the pain.

The old man gets angry and questions the doctor about his ability and expertise. This angers the doctor, who asks the old man, "How can you say that I know nothing and I am at fault for the pain in your leg?"

The old man innocently replies, "It is quite obvious you are wrong. My other leg is of the same age too, but has no pain at all!"

Announcing About Part-2

We will be soon available with the part 2

9 798888 692356

Printed by Libri Plureos GmbH in Hamburg,
Germany